AF372182

This book
belongs to:
___________________

___________________

___________________

___________________

First published 2023 with an exclusive licence from the authors to CHEETAH® Purrrrrrr Publishing, an imprint of CHEETAH® Toys & More, LLC (CHEETAH®).

Contact us: 1-860-781-1276, 1-876-909-6311 (WhatsApp),
info@mycheetahacademy.com;  paulettetrowers@yahoo.com

ISBN 13: 979-8-3303-3021-8
ISBN 10: 8-3303-3021-8

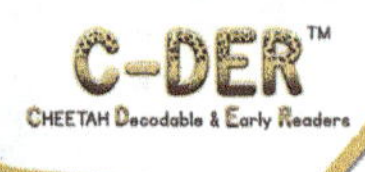


# Dear CHEETAH® family:

Our little books were specially created to help our early readers master their decoding skills and build reading fluency. The repetitive use of high-frequency words, word families, decodable words, rhymes, and vivid illustrations facilitates this process. Our stories complement the objectives and content highlighted in the Jamaica Early Childhood Curriculum Guide and the Ministry of Education and Youth Grade I National Standards Curriculum.

In journeying through our series, our little ones will develop a deeper awareness of and appreciation for our Jamaican culture. Our books also have universal appeal, as any early reader can identify with the characters, events and subjects in our texts. Readers will get to enjoy the stories, build vocabulary, and exercise critical thinking by engaging in the activities at the end of each story.

Additionally, as a precursor to our series, or as a support to it, we've created a decodable 'sentence strip' book for the very young readers and those who require more scaffolding.

Happy reading!

## CHEETAH®

### Chasing and capturing your dreams with you.

C-DER™
CHEETAH Decodable & Early Readers


Every letter is like a shining gem in the treasure chest of words, waiting to be discovered. Let's go! Let's discover the shining gems of words!

# My decodable words:
can, Nan, glad, mad, fed, shed, Ted, them, stem, bus, Gus

# Letter sound:

- consonant sound /d/ in the initial, medial and final positions in words

# Word families: 'an,' 'ad', 'ed', 'em', 'us'

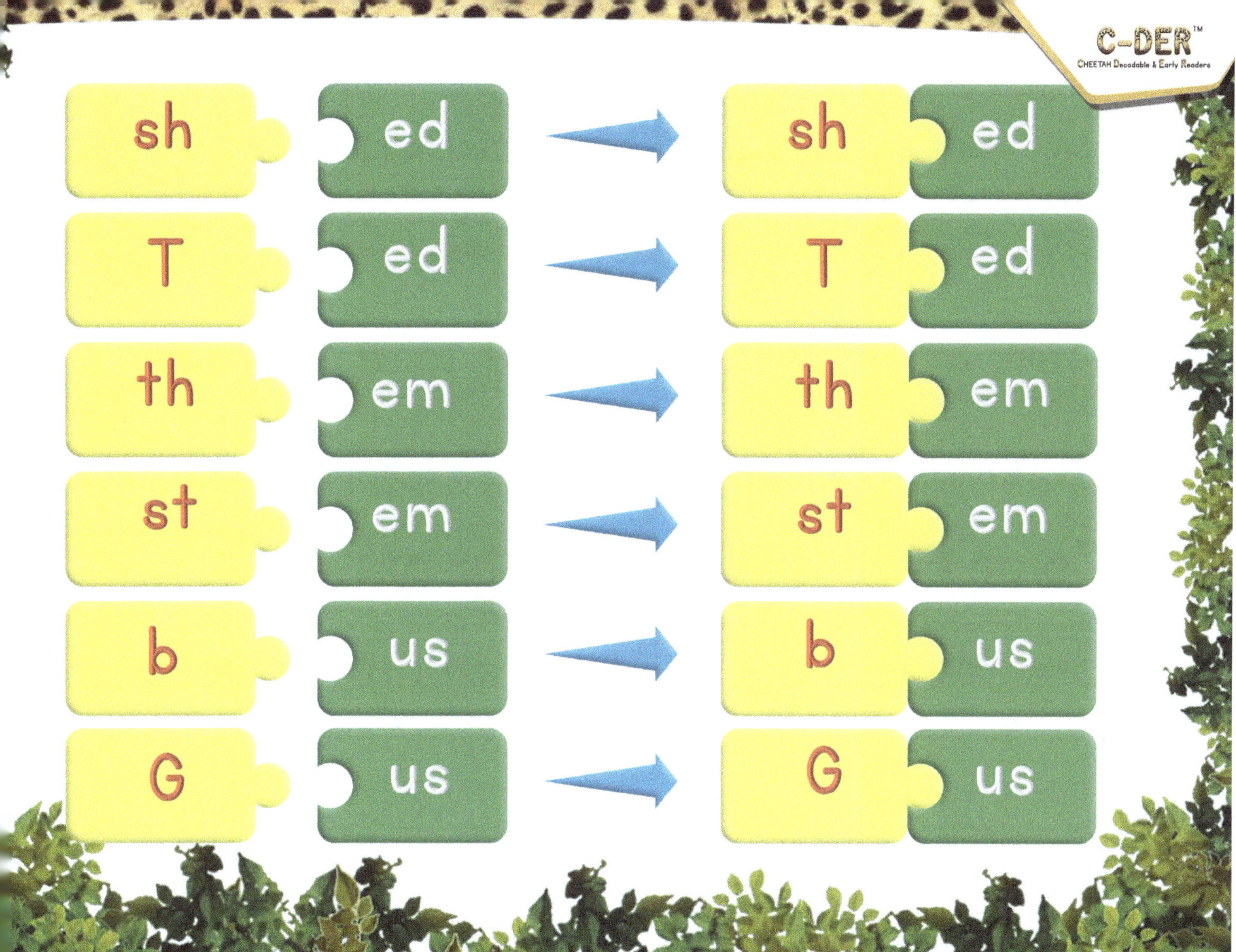

C-DER
CHEETAH Decodable & Early Readers
sh
ed
sh ed
T
ed
T ed
th
em
th em
st
em
st em
b
us
b us
G
us
G us

# Ted Disobeys

'Ted, after school, please take the bus.

Grandma is coming to visit us.

Come right away; there is lots to do.

Grandma and I will be waiting for you.'

C-DER
CHEETAH Decodable & Early Readers
2

C-DER™
CHEETAH Decodable & Early Readers
3

Ted says, 'Okay, Mom. I will see you both soon.
I will come home early this afternoon.'
He goes to school, and when the school day ends,
Ted stays in the yard to play with his friends.

C-DER
CHEETAH Decodable & Early Readers
School
5

When he looks at the time, he sees it is late.

Ted says 'bye' to his friends and runs out the gate.

Mom will not be happy that Ted missed the bus,

and that he stayed to play with his friends, Tim and Gus.

Ted runs and runs as fast as he can.

Far up the road, he sees Ken and Nan.

He tries his best to meet up with them...

Oops! He trips and holds on to a tree stem.

C-DER™
CHEETAH Decodable & Early Readers
8

He starts off again. He runs very fast.

He is now close to home at last.

He does not see when he steps on the paw

of the big brown dog that lives next door.

C-DER
CHEETAH Decodable & Early Readers
10

He was fast asleep by the front gate, where he always waits for his friend, Kate.

'Yelp! Yelp!' he says. He is not glad.

He runs after Ted. He is so mad!

C-DER
CHEETAH Decodable & Early Readers
12

Ted runs for his life.

He runs to their shed.

He pulls the door and bangs his head.

'Awch!' he says.

He waits for the dog to go.

How long will it take? He does not know.

C-DER
CHEETAH Decodable & Early Readers
14

Then he hears Mommy say, 'Are you in here, Ted?

The cats are still waiting to be fed.'

Ted says, 'I am sorry, Mommy.

I stayed to play.

I will never, ever again disobey.'

16

# Discussion and activities:

1. Have the children share instances when they disobeyed and got into some sort of trouble or difficulty. Ask them what they would do differently in that situation if they had a chance to do things over again.

2. Have the children identify the words with the target letter and sound.

3. Have the children make the sound of the target letter and identify rhyming words in the text.

4. Discuss the words *yelp, trips* and *bangs* as used in the context of the story.

5. Have the children read the text aloud.

1. How do you think Mommy discovered that Ted was in the shed?

........................................................................

2. What do you think would have happened if the dog had not chased Ted home?

........................................................................